A LOOK AT U.S. HISTORY

THE LEWIS AND CLARK EXPEDITION

BY BEATRICE HARRIS

Gareth Stevens PUBLISHING

CRASHCOURSE

Please visit our website, www.garethstevens.com. For a free color catalog of all our high-quality books, call toll free 1-800-542-2595 or fax 1-877-542-2596.

Library of Congress Cataloging-in-Publication Data

Names: Harris, Beatrice, author.
Title: The Lewis and Clark Expedition / Beatrice Harris.
Description: New York : Gareth Stevens Publishing, [2022] | Series: A look at U.S. history | Includes index. | Contents: An unexplored area -- The Corps of Discovery -- From Camp Dubois -- To Fort Mandan -- Sacagawea -- Through the Rockies -- Finding the Pacific -- The trip back -- A violent meeting -- Welcome back -- The expedition ends -- A timeline of the Lewis and Clark Expedition.
Identifiers: LCCN 2020013440 | ISBN 9781538266472 (library binding) | ISBN 9781538266458 (paperback) | ISBN 9781538266465 (set) | ISBN 9781538266489 (ebook)
Subjects: LCSH: Lewis and Clark Expedition (1804-1806)--Juvenile literature. | Clark, William, 1770-1838--Juvenile literature. | Lewis, Meriwether, 1774-1809--Juvenile literature. | West (U.S.)--Discovery and exploration--Juvenile literature.
Classification: LCC F592.7 .H2793 2022 | DDC 917.804/2--dc23
LC record available at https://lccn.loc.gov/2020013440

First Edition

Published in 2022 by
Gareth Stevens Publishing
111 East 14th Street, Suite 349
New York, NY 10003

Editor: Therese Shea

Photo credits: Series art Christophe BOISSON/Shutterstock.com; (feather quill) Galushko Sergey/Shutterstock.com; (parchment) mollicart-design/Shutterstock.com; cover, pp. 1, 25 Bettmann/Getty Images; p. 5 GraphicaArtis/Getty Images; p. 7 Burstein Collection/Corbis/VCG via Getty Images; p. 9 (both) courtesy of the Independence National Historical Park; p. 11 Ed Vebell/Getty Images; p. 13 (top) Heritage Art/Heritage Images via Getty Images; p. 13 (bottom) prospective56/iStock/Getty Images Plus; p. 15 Personal photograph taken at Montana State Capitol/Tungsten/Wikipedia.org; p. 17 (top) courtesy of the Library of Congress; pp. 17 (bottom), 29 (top) MPI/Getty Images; p. 19 (top) Mansell/Mansell/The LIFE Picture Collection via Getty Images; p. 19 (bottom) nick1803/iStock/Getty Images Plus; p. 21 (top) Visions of America/Education Images/Universal Images Group via Getty Images; p. 21 (bottom) Jean-Erick PASQUIER/Gamma-Rapho via Getty Images; p. 23 nicoolay/E+/Getty Images; p. 27 Raymond Boyd/Michael Ochs Archives/Getty Images; p. 29 (bottom) Wesley Hitt/Photographer's Choice RF/Getty Images.

Printed in the United States of America

CPSIA compliance information: Batch #CSGS22: For further information contact Gareth Stevens, New York, New York at 1-800-542-2595.

CONTENTS

An Unexplored Area 4
The Corps of Discovery 8
From Camp Dubois 10
To Fort Mandan 12
Sacagawea 14
Through the Rockies 16
Finding the Pacific 20
The Trip Back 22
A Violent Meeting 24
Welcome Back 26
The Expedition Ends 28
A Timeline of the Lewis and Clark Expedition 30
Glossary 31
For More Information 32
Index 32

Words in the glossary appear in **bold** type the first time they are used in the text.

AN UNEXPLORED AREA

At the beginning of the 1800s, the middle of North America wasn't well known to people in the young United States. In fact, it wasn't even part of the country yet. In 1803, the United States bought the land called the Louisiana Territory from France.

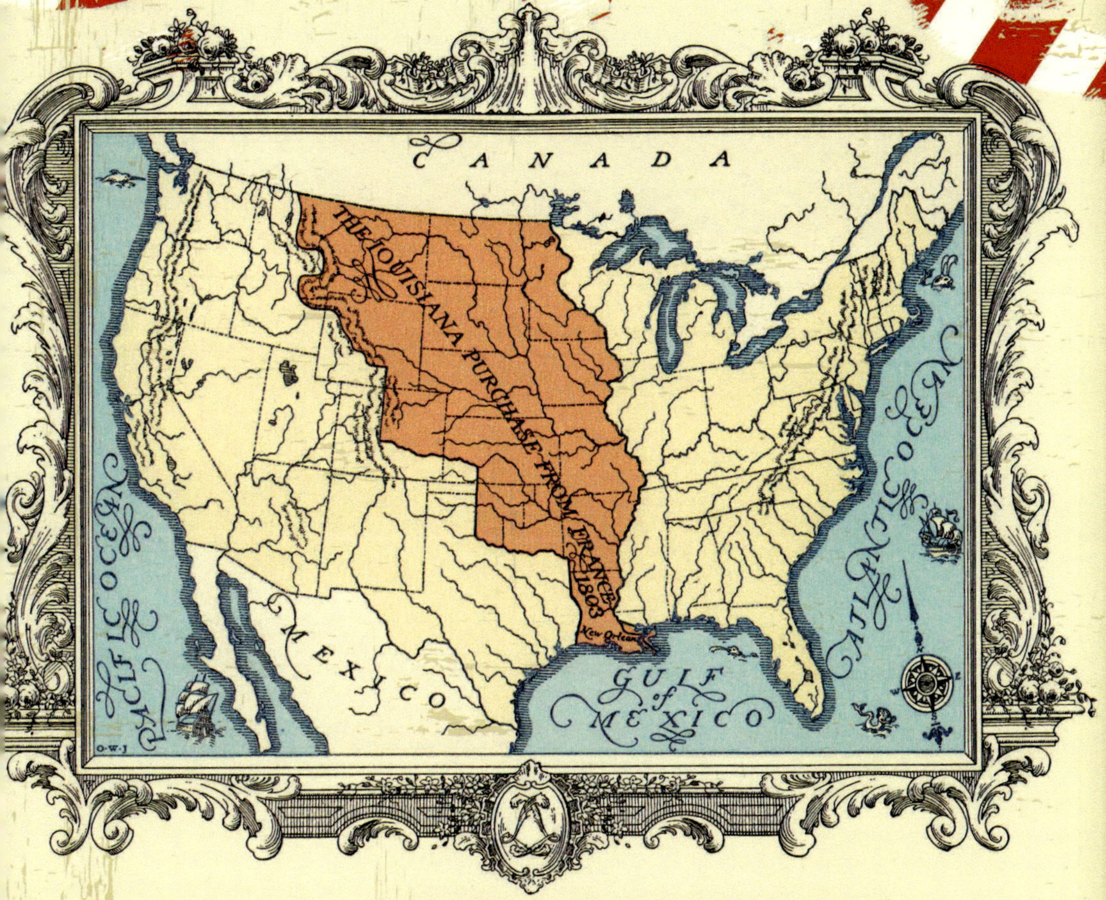

MAKE THE GRADE

All or part of these states came from the Louisiana Territory: Missouri, Arkansas, Iowa, North Dakota, South Dakota, Nebraska, Oklahoma, Louisiana, Kansas, Colorado, Wyoming, Montana, and Minnesota.

Before the Louisiana Territory became part of the United States, President Thomas Jefferson asked Congress for money for an **expedition**. He wanted to find a water route, or way, to the Pacific Ocean. He also wanted to begin trade with groups of Native Americans.

MAKE THE GRADE

The United States wanted to trade with Native Americans for furs. At that time, many animal furs had great value.

THOMAS JEFFERSON

THE CORPS OF DISCOVERY

Jefferson chose Meriwether Lewis to head the expedition. Lewis asked William Clark to help him lead. Both men had served in the army. They chose more men to join them. They called their group the **Corps** of Discovery.

MERIWETHER LEWIS

WILLIAM CLARK

MAKE THE GRADE

At first, the Corps of Discovery had around 45 people. One was an **enslaved** man named York.

FROM CAMP DUBOIS

William Clark trained the men of the expedition at Camp Dubois, which was north of St. Louis, Missouri. On May 14, 1804, the Corps of Discovery set out in boats on the Missouri River. They traveled about 15 miles (24 km) per day.

MAKE THE GRADE

The Corps used a large boat called a keelboat, shown here. Two smaller boats carried more supplies.

TO FORT MANDAN

The journey, or trip, wasn't easy. The Corps traveled through heat, rain, and cold. They had to deal with bugs and **injuries**. They spent the winter of 1804 to 1805 at Fort Mandan, which they built near today's Washburn, North Dakota.

CHARLES FLOYD

MAKE THE GRADE

The only person who died on the expedition was 22-year-old Charles Floyd. He was buried near today's Sioux City, Iowa. He might have died of **appendicitis**.

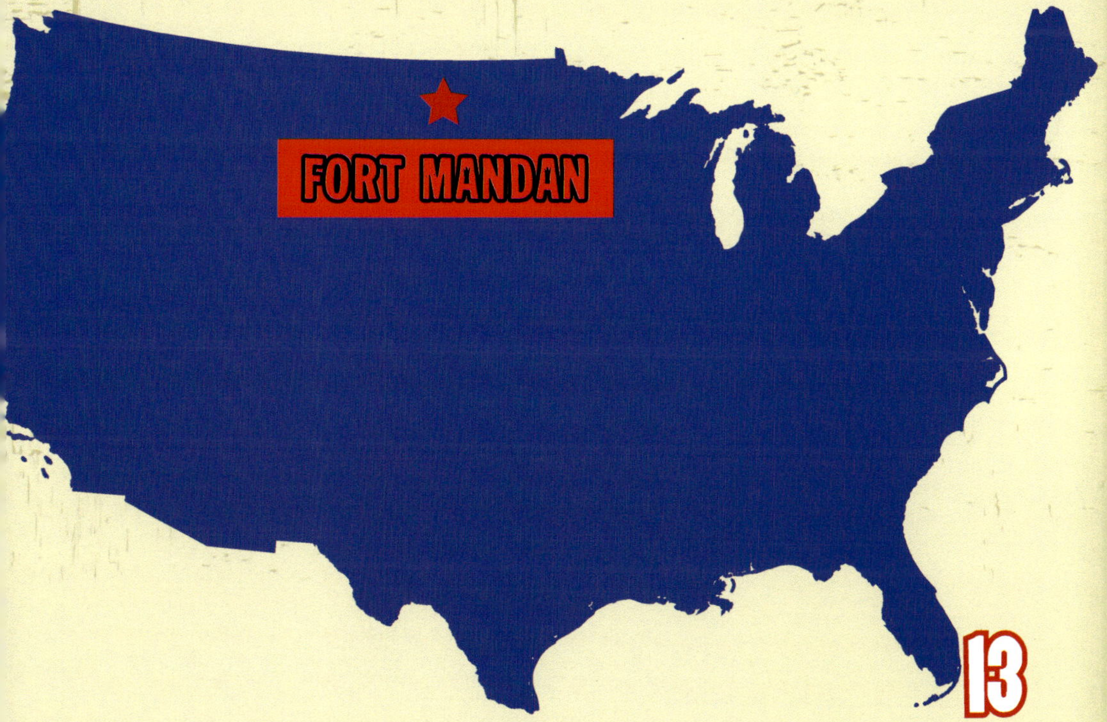

SACAGAWEA

The villages of the Mandan and Hidatsa Native Americans were near Fort Mandan. Here, Lewis and Clark hired a French-Canadian man named Toussaint Charbonneau to be an **interpreter** on the journey west. Charbonneau brought along his wife Sacagawea and their baby son.

MAKE THE GRADE

The Hidatsa had taken Sacagawea from her Shoshone family when she was about 12. She was about 16 when she met Lewis and Clark. She was very helpful on the journey.

THROUGH THE ROCKIES

In April 1805, the Corps of Discovery set out west again. They crossed today's state of Montana. When they got near the Rocky Mountains, they could no longer travel by boat on the Missouri River. They sailed the Jefferson River for a while.

MAKE THE GRADE

In April 1805, the Corps sent some men back to St. Louis with maps, reports, and live animals such as a prairie dog for President Jefferson.

In the Rocky Mountains, the Corps of Discovery came upon some Shoshone people. Sacagawea discovered that her brother Cameahwait was the chief. She helped the Corps buy horses from the Shoshone. The group almost **starved** traveling the Lolo Trail through the Bitterroot Mountains.

WILLIAM CLARK

MAKE THE GRADE

The Corps met Nez Percé people after traveling on the Lolo Trail for more than a week. The Nez Percé took care of the ill and tired Corps members.

BITTERROOT MOUNTAINS

FINDING THE PACIFIC

The Corps gave the Nez Percé their horses and built **canoes**. They traveled through **rapids** on the Clearwater River, then took the Snake River and the Columbia River. In November 1805, the Corps of Discovery finally reached the Pacific Ocean.

MAKE THE GRADE

The Corps spent the winter of 1805 to 1806 in Fort Clatsop. This was near today's Astoria, Oregon.

THE TRIP BACK

In March 1806, the Corps of Discovery began their trip home. Their work wasn't done. They decided to form groups. The groups traveled different routes on the way home so they could learn more about the land and people in the West.

MAKE THE GRADE

The groups planned to meet again where the Yellowstone and Missouri Rivers joined in North Dakota.

A VIOLENT MEETING

On the way east, the group led by Meriwether Lewis fought with Blackfeet Native Americans. They killed two Blackfeet. This **violence** was uncommon on the trip. The Corps met with almost 50 Native American groups over the journey. Most meetings were peaceful and friendly.

MAKE THE GRADE

Lewis and Clark gave gifts to the Native American peoples they met. They asked some to visit Washington, DC.

WELCOME BACK

On August 12, 1806, the Corps met up again. They returned Sacagawea and her family to the Mandan and Hidatsa villages. On September 23, they arrived in St. Louis, near where they had started. They had traveled more than 8,000 miles (12,875 km) in all.

MAKE THE GRADE

A statue in St. Louis, Missouri, shows Lewis and Clark and a dog. The dog, named Seaman, was part of the Corps of Discovery too.

THE EXPEDITION ENDS

Lewis and Clark didn't find a water route to the Pacific. However, they **accomplished** a lot. They made friends with many Native Americans. They **identified** plants and animals that most Americans didn't know about. Travelers used their maps of the West for years after the expedition.

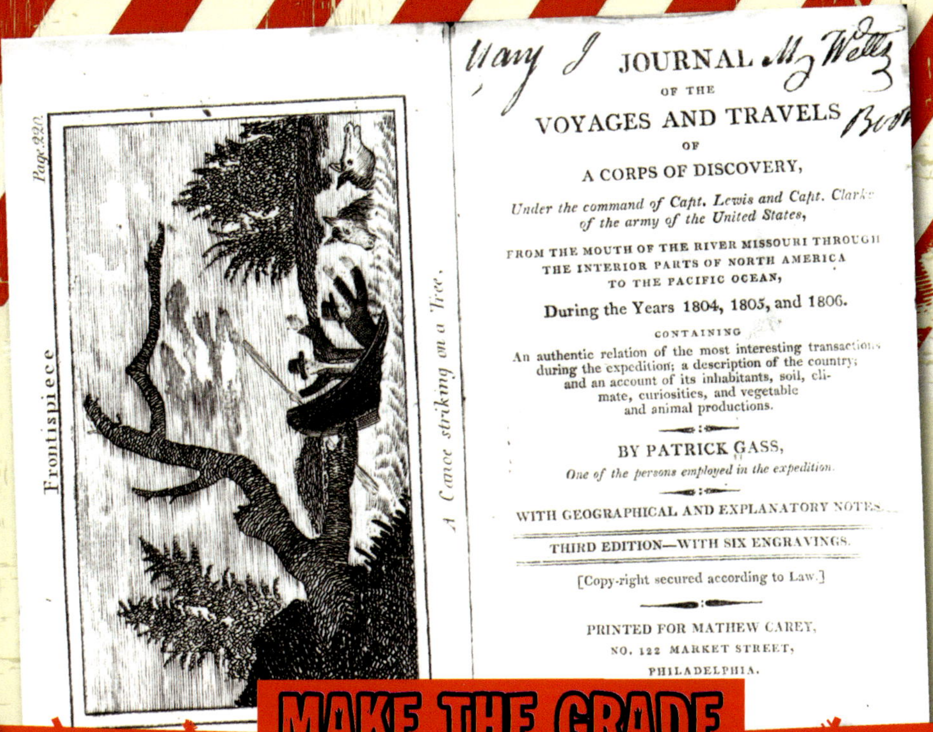

Page 220.

Frontispiece

A Canoe striking on a Tree.

JOURNAL
OF THE
VOYAGES AND TRAVELS
OF
A CORPS OF DISCOVERY,

Under the command of Capt. Lewis and Capt. Clarke of the army of the United States,

FROM THE MOUTH OF THE RIVER MISSOURI THROUGH THE INTERIOR PARTS OF NORTH AMERICA TO THE PACIFIC OCEAN,

During the Years 1804, 1805, and 1806.

CONTAINING

An authentic relation of the most interesting transactions during the expedition; a description of the country; and an account of its inhabitants, soil, climate, curiosities, and vegetable and animal productions.

BY PATRICK GASS,

One of the persons employed in the expedition.

WITH GEOGRAPHICAL AND EXPLANATORY NOTES.

THIRD EDITION—WITH SIX ENGRAVINGS.

[Copy-right secured according to Law.]

PRINTED FOR MATHEW CAREY,
NO. 122 MARKET STREET,
PHILADELPHIA.

MAKE THE GRADE

People still study the journals Lewis, Clark, and other Corps members wrote on the expedition. They can follow their famous route too.

A TIMELINE OF THE LEWIS AND CLARK EXPEDITION

JANUARY 18, 1803
President Thomas Jefferson asks Congress for money for an expedition west.

MAY 2, 1803
The United States buys the Louisiana Territory.

MAY 14, 1804
The Corps of Discovery, under leaders Lewis and Clark, leaves Camp Dubois near St. Louis, Missouri.

NOVEMBER 1804
The Corps builds a fort for the winter in today's North Dakota.

APRIL 7, 1805
The Corps sets out west again with interpreters Toussaint Charbonneau and Sacagawea.

AUGUST 1805
The Corps meets up with Shoshone people.

OCTOBER 16, 1805
The Corps reaches the Columbia River.

NOVEMBER 1805
The Corps reaches the Pacific Ocean and builds Fort Clatsop.

MARCH 23, 1806
The Corps begins the journey back east in a few groups.

AUGUST 12, 1806
The groups meet again at the Missouri River.

SEPTEMBER 23, 1806
The Corps of Discovery returns to St. Louis.

GLOSSARY

accomplish: to succeed in doing a task

appendicitis: a painful condition in which the organ called the appendix becomes swollen

canoe: a long, narrow boat often made by hollowing out a large log

corps: a group of soldiers trained for special service

enslaved: being "owned" by another person and forced to work without pay

expedition: a trip made for a certain purpose

identify: to find out the name or features of something

injury: harm or damage

interpreter: someone who can tell the meaning of another language

rapids: a rocky part of a river where the water moves fast

starve: to die from a lack of food

violence: the use of force to harm someone

FOR MORE INFORMATION

Books

Strand, Jennifer. *Lewis and Clark*. Minneapolis, MN: Abdo Zoom, 2017.

Yomtov, Nel. *Lewis and Clark Map the American West*. Minneapolis, MN: Bellwether Media, 2016.

Websites

Lewis and Clark
www.ducksters.com/biography/explorers/lewis_and_clark.php
Read quick facts about this famous pair.

Lewis and Clark Expedition
www.history.com/topics/westward-expansion/lewis-and-clark
Find out more about the journey.

Publisher's note to educators and parents: Our editors have carefully reviewed these websites to ensure that they are suitable for students. Many websites change frequently, however, and we cannot guarantee that a site's future contents will continue to meet our high standards of quality and educational value. Be advised that students should be closely supervised whenever they access the internet.

INDEX

Camp Dubois 10, 30
Corps of Discovery 8, 10, 11, 12, 16, 17, 18, 19, 20, 21, 22, 24, 26, 27, 29, 30
Fort Clatsop 21, 23, 30
Fort Mandan 12, 13, 14, 23
Jefferson, Thomas 6, 7, 17, 30
Louisiana Territory 4, 5, 6, 30
Native Americans 6, 7, 14, 24, 25, 28
Pacific Ocean 6, 20, 28, 30
Rocky Mountains 16, 18
Sacagawea 14, 15, 18, 26, 30
St. Louis 10, 17, 23, 26, 27, 30
York 9